Not by Bread Alone

Daily Reflections for Lent 2012

Bishop Robert F. Morneau

LITURGICAL PRESS

Collegeville, Minnesota

www.litpress.org

Nihil Obstat: Rev. Robert C. Harren, J.C.L., *Censor deputatus*.

Imprimatur: ✝ Most Rev. John F. Kinney, J.C.D., D.D., Bishop of St. Cloud, Minnesota, September 10, 2010.

Cover design by Ann Blattner. Photo: Hemera/Thinkstock.

ISSN: 1550-803X
ISBN: 978-0-8146-3310-6

Introduction

Between the Alpha and the Omega, between the beginning and the end, between our birth and our death, we experience life's journey. At the heart of that journey is our Christian faith. Made in the image and likeness of God and destined to share in the promise of eternal life, we are called to participate in the life of Christ and the gift of the Holy Spirit.

Lent has its Alpha and its Omega. We begin with Ash Wednesday and we end with the celebration of the great Easter mystery. The quality of the ending will depend, to a large extent, on how deeply we respond to Jesus' imperatives that we pray, fast, and give alms. During this liturgical season we are called to grow in our communication with God through meditation and contemplation. We are to practice asceticism, which is the spiritual exercise whereby through discipline we turn our will over to the will of God. And, because our spiritual journey is ultimately social, we turn to our sisters and brothers to assist them and for them to assist us in our need, be it physical, psychological, or spiritual.

As a pilgrim people we are not alone. Jesus promised us the gift of the Holy Spirit, the third person of the Blessed Trinity. It is the Holy Spirit who enlightens us to see God's concerns and purpose; it is the Holy Spirit who enkindles us to be on fire with compassion and love; it is the Holy Spirit who empowers us to discern God's will in our daily activities. So our praying, fasting, and almsgiving is something the Holy Spirit does in us as the principal agent, though, of course, our cooperation is essential.

Someone once wrote that "weak specification" is one of the greatest dangers of the spiritual life. We need to "nail things down"; we need to be specific regarding time and place if we are serious about our spiritual growth. One Lenten practice might be to take one corporal and one spiritual work of mercy and decide how we will live those two works of mercy over the next forty days. Here are those works of mercy:

Corporal Works of Mercy

> Feed the hungry
> Give drink to the thirsty
> Clothe the naked
> Shelter the homeless
> Visit the sick
> Ransom the captive
> Bury the dead

Spiritual Works of Mercy

> Instruct the ignorant
> Counsel the doubtful
> Admonish sinners
> Bear wrongs patiently
> Forgive offenses
> Comfort the afflicted
> Pray for the living and for the dead

By taking and living two of these works of mercy we deepen our participation in the life of Jesus, the servant of all. By doing what Jesus did, we are preparing ourselves to celebrate the great Easter mystery, our rising to new life in the risen Lord.

February 22: Ash Wednesday

Ambassadors for Christ

Readings: Joel 2:12-18; 2 Cor 5:20–6:2; Matt 6:1-6, 16-18

Scripture:
We are ambassadors for Christ,
  as if God were appealing through us.
We implore you on behalf of Christ,
  be reconciled to God. (2 Cor 5:20)

Reflection: Joel the prophet was an ambassador for God. His message, like that of St. Paul, was about reconciliation, that graced process of returning to the Lord. And how was this to take place? Joel, the Lord speaking through him, announces a time of fasting, a time to rend one's heart, a time to gather the people together and pray that the Lord might spare his people.

Pope John Paul II (1920–2005) followed the directions of the prophet Joel as he traveled around the world as an ambassador for God. While proclaiming a message of God's infinite love, the Holy Father also called all nations and his own beloved church to conversion. It is the mystery of sin that causes divisions and wars, hatred and chaos. It is the mystery of grace revealed in Jesus that brings about peace.

Besides the prophet Joel and Pope John Paul II, we are given the great model of St. Paul, who was one of the greatest ambassadors for Christ. His message on this first day of Lent is one of urgency: "Behold, now is a very acceptable time; behold, now is the day of salvation" (2 Cor 6:2). There is to be no delay in our response to the gospel imperatives to pray, to fast, and to give alms. When we follow Jesus' directives we foster the work of reconciliation.

In the 2009 biographical film *Invictus*, starring Morgan Freeman as South African president Nelson Mandela, we are given a contemporary example of reconciliation. Though imprisoned for twenty-seven years, Mandela called his people to forgiveness and not vengeance. It would appear that St. Paul's prayers from heaven and Jesus' mandate for peace were heeded.

Meditation: In what ways can you be an ambassador for Christ? In what sense is Lent a season of reconciliation? What examples of reconciliation have you witnessed?

Prayer: Lord God, the prophet Joel tells us that you are gracious and merciful, that you are slow to anger and rich in kindness, that you are relenting in punishment. May we experience these qualities during this season of Lent. May we live these qualities in our dealings with one another. Lord, "be merciful . . . for we have sinned" (Ps 51:3a).

February 23: Thursday after Ash Wednesday

A Stitch in Time . . .

Readings: Deut 30:15-20; Luke 9:22-25

Scripture:
For whoever wishes to save his life will lose it,
but whoever loses his life for my sake will save it.
What profit is there for one to gain the whole world
yet lose or forfeit himself? (Luke 9:24-25)

Reflection: "A stitch in time saves nine." The common understanding of this proverb is that if we take care of an issue immediately, we will not have to expand future effort. Stitching up a hole in a sweater prevents more unraveling.

Jesus had a philosophy about saving one's life, not the saving of nine future stitches. The Lord offers a paradox, saving means losing, and losing means saving. The mind struggles to unravel this enigma. More, the soul puzzles over how to live out this dying/rising pattern. Already on this second day of Lent we hear about Jesus' impending death. It will be by total surrender to the Father's will that Jesus will bring about the salvation of the world.

We need the gift of the Holy Spirit, especially the gifts of wisdom and discernment, if we are to figure out where true profit lies. Our instinctual drive to accumulate—to gain the whole world—is powerful, often addictive. We seem unable to ever get enough. The hunger for more power or possessions, for more pleasure and prestige, can be all consuming. If we yield to that temptation, we forfeit our very soul.

Lest we yield to this temptation, we need to do some soul stitching. At the first impulse toward greed (read—gaining more and more and more), we need a stitch of grace to preclude greed's vast power to unravel our integrity. For once we venture too far out in the ocean, the current will sweep us away and all will be lost. Moses understood this in his plea that his people choose life and not death. Moses was one of the first stitchers of souls.

Meditation: What turns loss into gain? What is the difference between economic and spiritual profit? What are the ways in which we can forfeit our very self?

Prayer: Loving God, give us the wisdom to distinguish between what is necessary and unnecessary, between our needs and our wants. In our weakness we struggle to put our time and energy into what really matters. Prevent us, gracious God, from forfeiting our souls by yielding to the cotton candy of life.

The "How" of Fasting

Readings: Isa 58:1-9a; Matt 9:14-15

Scripture:
This, rather, is the fasting that I wish:
   releasing those bound unjustly,
   untying the thongs of the yoke;
Setting free the oppressed,
   breaking every yoke;
Sharing your bread with the hungry. (Isa 58:6-7a)

Reflection: Pray! Fast! Give alms! It is one thing to be given these commands; it is another to know "how" to implement them. In dealing with prayer, Jesus taught his disciples the Our Father. In instructing the disciples on almsgiving, Jesus told the parable of the widow who gave her last mite. Isaiah comes along today to inform us on the "how" of fasting according to God's design. Knowing what to do is important; knowing how to do it is just as significant.

God is not concerned with sackcloth and ashes. Rather, the divine concern is how our mortification impacts the oppressed and homeless, the naked and hungry. Obviously, there is room for personal asceticism, be it the denial of food or the sacrifice of our time. We need to keep our house in order and not become dissipated. But the end of fasting and prayer and almsgiving is oneness, the building up of the community through deeds of justice and peace.

Timing is another issue in the "how" of fasting. It would be inappropriate to fast and mourn at a wedding celebration. Jesus gave us a great example in Cana of Galilee of rejoicing with those who rejoice and providing more than enough wine for the wedding guests. It is in times of loss and in facing our sinfulness that we need to embrace penance, the best penance being that of helping others.

Thomas Merton maintained that through penance the eye of both one's conscience and one's reason is cleared. Indeed, cleared enough to see our hurting sisters and brothers and reach out to them.

Meditation: What type of fasting are you doing this Lent? In what sense does discipline of the body impact on our dealings with our neighbor? What is the relationship between fasting and the call to do the works of justice and charity?

Prayer: Lord Jesus, you taught your disciples how to pray. Teach us how to fast, to fast in such a way that your Father's will might be done. Give us the wisdom to discern what true fasting is and the courage to put it into practice.

The Vocation Question

Readings: Isa 58:9b-14; Luke 5:27-32

Scripture:
Jesus saw a tax collector named Levi sitting at the customs
     post.
He said to him, "Follow me."
And leaving everything behind, he got up and followed him.
     (Luke 5:27-28)

Reflection: The vocation question is intriguing. God calls us
in a variety of ways. Our challenge is to be attentive and dis-
cerning, listening for the stirring of the Spirit and then responding promptly. Given the complexity of our times and the
rapidity of change, listening to the voice of God is difficult.

Levi's call was unique. Eyeball to eyeball with Jesus, the
tax collector heard those transforming words: "Follow me."
Interestingly, what we hear next is that Levi is throwing a
big party and a large crowd has gathered. Apparently, Levi
still had his house and plenty of food to share. His "leaving
everything" took some time. But leave it he did as he became
a disciple of Jesus, the very essence of "following" the Lord.

Our beautiful responsorial refrain—"Teach me your way,
O Lord, that I may walk in your truth" (Ps 86:11ab)—would
make a fitting prayer all the way through Lent (and beyond).
We need to be instructed in our vocation, in walking the way

of Jesus, the way of love, compassion, and forgiveness. More, we need to have the truth revealed to us, the truth of the dignity of every single human person, the truth that we need forgiveness of our sins, the truth that the Holy Spirit dwells within us. Only when we come in touch with the truth can we exercise authentic freedom.

According to the council fathers of Vatican II, the universal vocation is holiness. Before we respond to the single or married life, before we become a doctor or a farmer, before we feel called to priesthood or religious life, we are all called to the perfection of love, that is, the essence of holiness. St. Therese of Lisieux, a Doctor of the Church, says it well: "My vocation is to love."

C. S. Lewis believed that several things helped to provide "a tolerable index" of one's vocation: one's talents, one's upbringing, one's circumstance. To that we would surely add the proddings and nudges of the Holy Spirit.

Meditation: What does Christ's imperative "follow me" mean to you? How do you follow in the way of Jesus? What is your understanding of the notion that everyone's vocation is the call to holiness?

Prayer: Providential God, teach us your ways. Through the gift of the Holy Spirit may we discern daily what you ask of us. Give us the gift of wisdom to know your truth; give us the gift of courage to do your will.

The Nearness of the Kingdom

Readings: Gen 9:8-15; 1 Pet 3:18-22; Mark 1:12-15

Scripture:
After John had been arrested,
   Jesus came to Galilee proclaiming the gospel of God:
   "This is the time of fulfillment.
The kingdom of God is at hand.
Repent, and believe in the gospel." (Mark 1:14-15)

Reflection: By abstaining forty long days from earthly food, Jesus consecrated through his fast the pattern of our Lenten observance and, by overturning all the snares of the ancient serpent, taught us to cast out the leaven of malice, so that, celebrating worthily the Paschal Mystery, we might pass over at last to the eternal paschal feast. The liturgy opens up for us various aspects of God's kingdom, this state in which God rules, guides, and reigns in our hearts and, hopefully, in our world.

One dimension of the kingdom is its nearness. Indeed, it is at hand. Whenever we witness the poor being tended, the transgressor forgiven, the enslaved freed, we are seeing the kingdom enacted. Whenever war turns to peace, hatred to love, and death to life, the kingdom is there. So, the kingdom is not far off in distant hills or down the centuries. It is here and now, wherever and whenever we are doing God's will.

A second dimension of the kingdom is that its realization is primarily the work of the Holy Spirit. True, we are called to be instruments in the building of the kingdom, but the Holy Spirit is always the principal agent. Our Lenten prayer should be one of invoking the Spirit to come into our minds and hearts so that we might come into contact with the truth and experience God's love. Then we venture forth to do the works of justice and peace, knowing full well both the origin and energy behind which all that we do is accomplished.

A third aspect of God's kingdom is joy. St. Paul's classic line in his letter to the Romans should be engraved on our hearts: "[T]he kingdom of God is not a matter of food and drink, but of righteousness, peace and joy in the holy Spirit" (Rom 14:17). But this is a muted joy for we know that many individuals and nations reject God's reign, thereby throwing themselves and others into darkness and sadness. This fact, however, should never prevent us from truly rejoicing in God's governance in our lives.

Meditation: When you pray "thy kingdom come," what does that mean to you? During this season of Lent, how can you further God's kingdom?

Prayer: Jesus, you proclaimed boldly that your Father's kingdom was near at hand. Help us to see the workings of your Holy Spirit; empower us to cooperate with your Spirit in doing our part in furthering your reign. Fill us with your justice, peace, and joy.

Expectations: Divine and Human

Readings: Lev 19:1-2, 11-18; Matt 25:31-46

Scripture:
"Then the king will say to those on his right,
　'Come, you who are blessed by my Father.
Inherit the kingdom prepared for you from the foundation
　of the world.'" (Matt 25:34)

Reflection: God has expectations of us just as we do of God. Nor is it difficult to know what those expectations are. Scripture reveals to us that at the heart of the divine design is a call to service and sacrifice. We are called to be for others even to the point of total self-sacrifice. God expects us to feed the hungry, clothe the naked, provide shelter for the homeless. What we expect of God is another matter.

The atheist expects nothing since there is no God. We are alone in the universe, indeed, lost in the cosmos. Any appeal to some transcendent reality is absurd and meaningless. There is no ultimate rationale for our human existence.

The agnostic, although claiming that we cannot know, hedges his bets. Though there is no discernable evidence for faith claims, there are "signals of transcendence," as the sociologist Peter Berger maintained. Such things as order, hope, and humor point to something or Someone beyond the borders of our narrow materialism.

And the religious person? Depending on one's tradition, the traditions of the great world religions, the expectations of God will vary. For the Christian, whose mind and heart is informed by revelation, faith, and reason, God is a God of love and mercy. Therefore we can expect that we are the beloved of God and that we are the subject of his merciful forgiveness. More, this God is creator, redeemer, and sanctifier and thus we can expect a continual influx of life, an abiding healing presence, and a constant source of fire and light through the gift of the Holy Spirit.

Unlike the character in Thomas Hardy's *The Return of the Native*—"As for Thomasin, I never expected much from her; and she has not disappointed me."—we expect as much from God as God expects from us. Our Lenten task is to figure out those expectations so that we do not disappoint our faithful God.

Meditation: What are your expectations of God and of yourself? How have these expectations changed over the years? How do you deal with disappointment?

Prayer: Merciful and loving God, send your Spirit into our hearts that we might know what you expect of us. And may that Holy Spirit empower us to live out those expectations. May our expectations of you be grounded in the mystery of Jesus, the one who came to give his all for our salvation.

Praying with Absolute Attention

Readings: Isa 55:10-11; Matt 6:7-15

Scripture:
"This is how you are to pray:
Our Father who art in heaven,
    hallowed be thy name,
    thy Kingdom come,
thy will be done,
    on earth as it is in heaven." (Matt 6:9-10)

Reflection: In her spiritual autobiographical letter, Simone Weil (1909–43) tells of an experience she had in memorizing the Our Father in Greek. While praying the Lord's Prayer with absolute attention, Jesus was present to her in an intense way. Praying in that fashion changed the geography of her inner life.

There is no need to learn the Our Father in either Greek or Latin. English is sufficient, but as we pray we are challenged to give absolute attention to words and what they refer to. This is no easy task. Our monkey-minds tend to wander all over the place. The ability to give total concentration to each word and phrase demands not only effort but also the working of grace.

So what name are we to hallow? God is indeed our Father; God is our Creator; God is Love. The mystery of God is so deep that words can never capture the full depth of our Deity. Whatever the language, whatever specific word we use, what is foundational to all prayer is reverence. We hallow our God as the source of life and all holiness. We reverence the God who is, who was, and who is to come. We hallow God by giving him glory and praise.

So what about the kingdom? Jesus tells us to pray that God's kingdom might rule not only our personal lives but also the entire world. God's kingdom comes when truth is spoken, love is expressed, justice is done, freedom is advanced. God's kingdom is present and manifest when there is an increase of love, joy, and peace.

So what is God's will? In praying the Our Father we realize that we are to be agents of God's will, ambassadors of Christ helping in the work of reconciliation.

St. Francis de Sales maintained that the best prayer is the one in which we are not thinking about ourselves but rather are totally occupied with God. The Our Father is our best prayer when we pray it with absolute attention.

Meditation: What role does the Our Father have in your spirituality? How attentive are you in your prayer life?

Prayer: Lord Jesus, thank you for teaching us how to pray. Continue to send forth your Spirit that we may taste every word and respond to every moment of grace.

Jonah: God's Man

Readings: Jonah 3:1-10; Luke 11:29-32

Scripture:
The word of the LORD came to Jonah a second time:
"Set out for the great city of Nineveh,
and announce to it the message that I will tell you."
(Jonah 3:1)

Reflection: There are two dimensions in the life of every prophet, apostle, and disciple of the Lord. One concerns their very being, who they are; the other deals with their ministry, their being sent on a specific mission. Jonah was called by the Lord to undertake a perilous journey. Though not without struggle, Jonah became "God's man." And then came the assignment: call the king and the city of Nineveh to conversion, to a change of heart.

Thomas Merton (1915–68) once made this comment about saints and preaching: "For the saint preaches sermons by the way he walks the way he stands and the way he sits down and the way he picks things up and holds them in his hand." Jonah's preaching was not just a matter of words, though the forty-day warning carried much fear and trembling, but it also involved the person of Jonah. Something radiated from his being that brought credibility to the message. The three-day walk through Nineveh gave many people the opportunity to observe this prophet.

In one of his essays, John Henry Cardinal Newman questioned the effectiveness of preaching. One might wonder how Newman reacted to Jonah's mission. From all appearances, it was a most effective ministry that brought the king (and "man and beast") to don sackcloth and ashes. Any preaching that can do that is powerful indeed. Add to this the fact that God also decided not to inflict harm on the people of Nineveh and you have a truly influential preacher.

God is always calling and sending. All of us on this Lenten journey continue to be called to discipleship and sent to spread the good news of God's love and mercy. It all began in baptism—this call and sending—and it continues on a daily basis. May our response be as sincere and as effective as that of Jonah.

Meditation: How do you hear God's daily call? What is the specific mission (ministry) that God has assigned to you? How do you evaluate your effectiveness?

Prayer: Just as you called and sent Jonah, Lord, you call and send us. May we feel deep within our being the invitation to discipleship. May our energies be directed toward the building of your kingdom. Make us good preachers, both in word and in action.

Stones and Snakes / Bread and Fish

Readings: Esth C:12, 14-16, 23-25; Matt 7:7-12

Scripture:
Which one of you would hand his son a stone
   when he asked for a loaf of bread,
      or a snake when he asked for fish? (Matt 7:9-10)

Reflection: Queen Esther, an orphan and alone, asked God to save her and her handmaids from a lion. She pleaded with God that her sorrows be turned into gladness. She prayed for persuasive words with which to confront her enemy. This woman of prayer had deep faith, believing that what she asked for would be granted, what she sought would be found. Would that our Lenten faith and prayer be as deep as hers.

Jesus, in speaking about prayer, uses figures of speech to instruct the disciples regarding the nature of his Father. The images of a stone and a snake, the metaphors of a loaf of bread and fish clarify once and for all that just as a responsible parent would never deny a child the necessities of life, so God will give us the good things necessary for our salvation. Stones do not nourish; snakes can be dangerous. By contrast, bread and fish sustain our journey.

During this season of Lent we have a golden opportunity to reflect on how well or poorly we image our God, this God of all life and holiness. God is a Giver, endowing us with life and love and mercy. Made in the image and likeness of this God, we are to give life, love, and mercy to others, sharing the gifts we have received. Today's gospel imperative from Matthew should be etched on our hearts: "Do to others whatever you would have them do to you" (Matt 7:12a).

One of the greatest obstacles on our faith journey is an immature concept of God. To misconceive God is ruinous to our prayer life. The God revealed in Jesus is a God who is totally for us, giving us bread and fish, love and mercy, salvation and peace. Our God is not a God of stones and snakes, of vengeance and hatred, of death and doom. Esther and the disciples came to know this and by so doing, experienced the joy and peace of faith.

Meditation: What are you seeking and asking from God? What is your image of God and how has that image changed over the years? In what ways has God nourished you on your faith journey?

Prayer: God of bread and fish, God of love and mercy, come to our aid. Like Esther, we face enemies within and without. We stand in need of your daily assistance and nourishment. May the Eucharist become ever more deeply the source of our life.

Turn! Turn! Turn!

Readings: Ezek 18:21-28; Matt 5:20-26

Scripture:
Thus says the Lord GOD:
If the wicked man turns away from all the sins he has
    committed,
  if he keeps all my statutes, and does what is right and
      just,
  he shall surely live, he shall not die. (Ezek 18:21)

Reflection: In 1959, the folksinger Pete Seeger wrote his popular song "Turn! Turn! Turn!" The lyrics were taken from the third chapter of the book of Ecclesiastes wherein the author speaks of the fact that there is a season for everything. The theme of "turning" is central to Lent, our liturgical season of conversion and change of heart.

Ezekiel the prophet delivers God's message about vice and virtue, about wickedness and goodness. Each of us must decide what road we will walk down. If it is the path of wickedness, the Scriptures tell us to turn around and return to our God lest we die. More, if the virtuous person turns from good deeds and hikes down the trail of darkness and sin, the person will forfeit his or her life. This is serious stuff; this is a matter of life and death with the note of eternity attached.

Jesus continues the conversation. To enter God's kingdom, our righteousness cannot be limited to adhering to laws and statutes, important as they are. More is demanded. This is where the going gets rough: we must forgive and be reconciled with one another. If not, how can we expect to be reconciled to God? Much grace is needed here because our human weakness and our proclivity to hold grudges are so great. Jesus set the example in forgiving those who tortured and killed him.

The Carmelite poet Jessica Powers, in her brilliant poem "The House at Rest," raises the question of what it is that brings peace to our dwellings, that puts our houses at rest. Very simply: "Virtue it is that puts the house at rest." This is the message of Ezekiel; this is the message of Jesus. By turning away from vice and wickedness, by turning to virtue and goodness, we experience life and love, joy and peace. There is a season for everything and our Lenten season is one of turning again to the Lord.

Meditation: What is your understanding of virtue? Locate Pete Seeger's song "Turn! Turn! Turn!" and then read Ecclesiastes, chapter 3. Is reconciliation a matter of life and death to you and to the community?

Prayer: Lord, send your Spirit into our hearts and into our world. Give us the grace to be reconciled to you and to one another; grant us the virtues we need to further your kingdom. Come, Holy Spirit, come.

Indiscriminate Love and Prayer

Readings: Deut 26:16-19; Matt 5:43-48

Scripture:
". . . love your enemies,
  and pray for those who persecute you,
  that you may be children of your heavenly Father,
  for he makes his sun rise on the bad and the good,
  and causes rain to fall on the just and the unjust."
    (Matt 5:44b-45)

Reflection: Sun and rain are indiscriminate. Would that our love and prayer were the same. Loving the lovable and praying for those near and dear to us are not difficult activities. The test comes when we have been hurt or rejected, when someone has done us in, when the scars are not yet healed. It is at these crossroads that discipleship will be challenging.

In wartimes, nations have experienced a "fifth column," a group of people within its boundaries that will assist the attacking forces. Another interpretation of "fifth column" is an enemy within. When Jesus speaks of loving your enemies, sometimes that means we must love ourselves and pray for that part of us that is destructive. Psychologists and spiritual directors are well aware that self-acceptance and, even more, self-forgiveness are extremely difficult.

Grace is needed to love the enemy within and without, to pray for persecutors within and without. And that grace is as ubiquitous as the sun and the rain. The Holy Spirit is the principal agent of our prayer and of our love. It is the Holy Spirit who softens our heart and illumines our mind. The Holy Spirit is God's sun and God's rain, refreshing, healing, and giving us a whole new life.

In the end, none of us can claim to be a "just" person. All of us, at some level, have failed in our duties and obligations to God, to one another, and to our nation. So when good things happen to the "unjust," let us rejoice for we are in that same category. God's love is not discriminatory. Whoever is open and receptive can receive God's tender mercies. But there is a catch. That mercy must be passed on to others. The gift given is not simply for oneself. If we stop the flow, eventually our love will diminish and our prayer might well become ineffective.

Meditation: Who are your enemies, within and without? How has God's sun and rain poured down on you? Have you passed it on to others?

Prayer: On the cross, Lord Jesus, you asked forgiveness for your persecutors. In the Garden of Gethsemane, you loved Judas even in the act of his betrayal. Send us your Spirit of compassion and kindness lest we fail to love and pray for our enemies.

Three Tents

Readings: Gen 22:1-2, 9a, 1-13, 15-18; Rom 8:31b-34; Mark 9:2-10

Scripture:
Then Peter said to Jesus in reply,
 "Rabbi, it is good that we are here!
Let us make three tents:
 one for you, one for Moses, and one for Elijah."
  (Mark 9:5)

Reflection: Two significant words in our lexicon are "here" and "now." The "here" deals with the "where" question, with space and geography. The "now" deals with the "when" question, with time and temporality.

Peter, that intuitive and impetuous disciple, got it right: how good to be with the Lord on the mountain. In that sacred space, Peter, James, and John were given a special revelation as they realized that Jesus was the very embodiment of the Law (Moses) and the Prophets (Elijah). No wonder Peter yearned for that experience to continue and not be transitory. By building three tents, perhaps that moment of grace would perdure.

One wonders if Abraham would dare say that it was good for him and his son to be in the land of Moriah. No mention here of building a tent. No ecstasy, but rather a testing of the most severe nature—being asked to sacrifice one's most precious possession. What we witness here in Abraham's obedience is the imperative in the gospel, namely, that all of us have to listen to God and do his bidding.

St. Irenaeus describes the will of God as the "Father's good pleasure." God's good pleasure is that all be saved: Isaac, Peter, James, John, you, and me. That salvation comes from our fidelity to the Law and the Prophets, from our fidelity to the person of Jesus. It is in those three tents—the Law, the Prophets, Jesus—where we hear about God's will and where we are given the grace to live lives of obedient faith.

St. Paul knew those three tents and realized the limitations of the Mosaic Law and the wisdom of the prophets. But most of all, Paul knew about the incredible grace of God's love and mercy in Jesus, the only true source of redemption. Paul experienced, like Peter, James, and John, that God is for us and not against us. More, Jesus—here and now!—intercedes for us at God's right hand. No need to build tents when the Holy Spirit already dwells in the depth of our souls.

Meditation: What evidence do you have in your life that God is for you? How important are the Prophets, the gospels, and the Mosaic Law (especially the Decalogue) to you?

Prayer: Gracious and loving Father, draw us into your presence, we who wander and drift far from your good pleasure. Give us ears to listen to your Son; give us a heart, at once compassionate and humble, to follow in his way. We make our prayer through Jesus, our savior, brother, and friend.

The Curé of Ars

Readings: Dan 9:4b-10; Luke 6:36-38

Scripture:
"Give and gifts will be given to you;
   a good measure, packed together, shaken down, and
      overflowing,
  will be poured into your lap.
For the measure with which you measure
  will in return be measured out to you." (Luke 6:38)

Reflection: Two of God's outstanding gifts are mercy and compassion. To be forgiven and to receive affective understanding can transform our lives. No wonder the prophet Daniel calls God great and awesome, a God who is faithful to his merciful covenant. That covenant is a two-way street. Just as God offers us his love, we are to offer our obedience and keep the commandments, especially the commandment of love.

Sin thwarts God's will. When we are unloving, when we lack mercy and compassion, when we turn our backs on others in need, we distance ourselves from experiencing God's abiding love. Lent is a season of repentance that calls us, in honesty and courage, to deal with the darkness of our souls and of our culture.

Through the sacrament of reconciliation the grace of God's mercy is poured into our laps. St. John Vianney (1786–1859), the Curé of Ars, was given an extraordinary gift as a confessor. He spent countless hours in the confessional, reading with compassion the souls of penitents and extending to them the mercy of Christ. This humble priest knew himself to be forgiven. Thus, no condemnation of others, no harsh judgment, no holding back on love. Though St. John Vianney had to struggle with theological studies, he had no struggle in making God's divine mercy present and manifest.

It is somewhat of a paradox that the more we give in the area of spiritual matters, the more room is created for the next influx of grace. It is when we hang on to a blessing or grace, keeping it primarily for ourselves, that difficulties arise. Our God is a Giver; we are made in God's image and likeness. Our God is a God of compassion; we too are to be merciful and compassionate.

Meditation: What gifts has God given you? What are the standards and criteria that you use in assessing your own spiritual growth and that of others? Do you find it paradoxical that the more you give of graces received, the more you receive?

Prayer: Faithful and merciful God, guide us in your ways. Never allow us to condemn; always help us to be merciful. As you have seen fit to forgive us, may we forgive others. As you have formed a covenant with us, may we live in loving relationships with our sisters and brothers.

Setting Things Right

Readings: Isa 1:10, 16-20; Matt 23:1-12

Scripture:
Wash yourselves clean!
Put away your misdeeds from before my eyes;
    cease doing evil; learn to do good.
Make justice your aim: redress the wronged,
    hear the orphan's plea, defend the widow. (Isa 1:16-17)

Reflection: The teacher or parent who says, "Don't do as I do, do as I say," lacks both credibility and authenticity. Words and preaching are one thing; example and modeling are another. Jesus took on the scribes and Pharisees, not for their teaching, but for their failure to live the instructions given by Moses. Although the pragmatism proclaimed by William James has its defects, there is a strong element of pragmatism in the gospel and in the prophets.

By pragmatism I mean doing the truth, not just proclaiming it. Isaiah the prophet took on the leaders of Sodom and the people of Gomorrah. They must change their attitudes and behaviors. God is always willing to forgive but that forgiveness cannot be experienced if we cling to evil, fail to help those in need, neglect the deeds of justice, refuse to embrace humility. This is a call to obedience; this is a call to a life of service; this is a call to repentance.

God understands our human struggle and approaches us with compassion and mercy. One of the most beautiful passages in all of Scripture is in our first reading today: "Come now, let us set things right, / says the LORD: / Though your sins be like scarlet, / they may become white as snow; / Though they be crimson red, / they may become white as wool" (Isa 1:18). God takes the initiative in approaching us this Lent with the aim of setting things right. Our scarlet, red sins will become white as snow and wool. This is more than poetry; this is God's promise of forgiveness. We need but obey.

Our responsorial refrain—"To the upright I will show the saving power of God" (Ps 50:23b)—reminds us again that salvation and righteousness are of one piece. In Jesus, God's redemptive power is made present. When we embrace a life of discipleship, following in the way of Jesus, we will walk in the Lord's righteous path.

Meditation: Are there any things in your life that you "preach" but do not practice? What is the connection between right living and salvation? What is your understanding of pragmatism and what is its relationship to truth?

Prayer: Saving God, direct our steps in the ways of justice and peace. Turn our scarlet sins into blinding white snow; turn our weaknesses into instruments of your grace. Too easily we lose our way. Come, Lord Jesus, and set things right once and for all.

Desires, Longings, Yearnings

Readings: Jer 18:18-20; Matt 20:17-28

Scripture:
"Rather, whoever wishes to be great among you shall be
    your servant;
  whoever wishes to be first among you shall be your
      slave." (Matt 20:26-27a)

Reflection: Authors disagree about our deepest wishes, longings, yearnings, desires. Fr. Ronald Rolheiser would say that
the two basic longings are for intimacy and transcendence.
Robert Kegan maintains that our yearnings for inclusion and
distinctness are most fundamental. Nikos Kazantzakis' two
deepest desires were for freedom and sanctity. Maybe these
authors might see this just as a matter of semantics and that
ultimately they are speaking about the same thing; maybe
not. Regardless, all would agree that no one is exempt from
profound longings.

The mother of James and John had a wish: high places in
Jesus' kingdom for her sons. Jesus then explains the condi-
tions for the fulfillment of that wish: a life of total self-giving.
The other ten disciples express indignation over a political
move that could result in a lower place in the kingdom for
them. At this point, the Lord clarifies the meaning of greatness in the Father's reign. Jesus then concludes by describing

his longing: that his disciples follow in his way of being a servant and a ransom for many.

Jeremiah, a servant and prophet of God, is under attack. His enemies are noting every word so as to entrap him, just as the enemies of Jesus were looking for ways to trip him up and kill him. What was going on in the heart of Jeremiah? What were his wishes and longings and desire? Intimacy and transcendence? Inclusion and distinctness? Freedom and sanctity? Greatness? We don't know for sure but one thing arises from Jeremiah's prayer: that good might prevail. So maybe in the end our deepest longing, often unconscious and inarticulate, is for the good to win out. That is to say, that love, the supreme good, might be both received and given. It is here that universal agreement may be achieved.

Meditation: What are your deepest longings? What role does service play in your life? Reflect on the great people you know. If alive, send them a note.

Prayer: Lord Jesus, purify our desires. Help us to long for what really matters and help us to be done with things that are insignificant and of no consequence. Too often we waste our precious time and energy on inane entertainment, dead-end projects, and trivial conversation. Send your Spirit to enlighten us to see what really matters.

Our Physicians: Human and Divine

Readings: Jer 17:5-10; Luke 16:19-31

Scripture:
I, the LORD, alone probe the mind
  and test the heart,
To reward everyone according to his ways,
  according to the merit of his deeds. (Jer 17:10)

Reflection: Those who have had an annual physical exam experience firsthand what probing is all about. The doctor, with instruments that would intimidate the most courageous of us, pushes and prods, invades and intrudes until not a single corpuscle is left untouched. And all this for the sake of health! How much more intense and revelatory is the probing by our God who, bypassing somewhat our bodies, goes for the mind and heart. Therein reside the thoughts and feelings that shape our daily deeds.

The rich man in today's gospel, clad in the finest garment and having access to the finest food, is in serious trouble. Though his body is well provided for, something is mortally awry. He lacks a social conscience. Those who have no clothing or shelter or food are absent from his radar screen. Upon death, the rich man experiences the consequences of his decisions: a life separated from God in eternity as his life was separated from his fellow creatures on this earth. His mind and heart, centered on self, reaped its fatal reward.

During Lent we are called to some degree of introspection. What do we think about: How compassionate is our heart? What deeds flow out of our conscience? The smallest grain of truth will reveal that all of us, without exception, have unredeemed areas in our mind and heart. We all stand in need of conversion and transformation. This is a painful process calling for no small courage. We are called to listen to Moses and the prophets. We are called to listen to Jesus and his teaching of the Beatitudes and the last judgment scene. In hearing and responding to these scriptural imperatives, we will enter into the grace of reconciliation.

In *The Scarlet Letter*, Nathaniel Hawthorne writes: "A man burdened with a secret should especially avoid the intimacy of his physician." Maybe there is another piece of wisdom: a person burdened with a secret will find peace and joy by encountering the Divine Physician, our merciful and loving and probing God.

Meditation: What are the secrets of your mind and heart? What does the Hawthorne quote say to you? Why is there such urgency in our Lenten season?

Prayer: Probing and loving God, look deeply into our minds and hearts. Heal us of all darkness and indifference, of all meanness and doubt. Give us a sense of hope and trust in your abiding, caring presence. Grant us your peace and joy.

The Ambiguity of World History

Readings: Gen 37:3-4, 12-13a, 17b-28a; Matt 21:33-43, 45-46

Scripture:
"When vintage time drew near,
  he [the landowner] sent his servants to the tenants to
      obtain his produce.
But the tenants seized the servants and one they beat,
  another they killed, and a third they stoned."
      (Matt 21:34-35)

Reflection: Fr. Karl Rahner, SJ, was one of the most brilliant theologians of the twentieth century. His teaching and writing influenced the documents of the Second Vatican Council as well as the thought of the theological community. In 1958 his book *On Prayer* was published, and, in one of the chapters, he raised this question: "Why is world history a swirl of stupidity, meanness and brutality?"

We might ask that same question of the Bible: why is the Bible filled with "a swirl of stupidity, meanness and brutality?" The story from Genesis is a violent drama: brothers plotting to kill a brother; hatred so great that Joseph's brothers refuse to look at him; they throw Joseph into a cistern and then sell him off for twenty pieces of silver. Mean! Stupid! Brutal!

Then we have Jesus' parable, yet another example of the swirl of violence in the human heart. Servants are sent by the landowner to obtain his portion of the harvest. What happens? Seizure, killing, stoning, even of the landowner's son. It's not a pretty picture, be it the events of world history or the stories of the Bible.

Yet there is more to world history and the Bible than this. Granted, we must not pass over the dark side of human freedom, yet world history and the Bible are filled with wisdom, kindness, and respect as well. The sea of darkness has above it an infinity of light and love. Herein lies our hope. God, who created this universe and our personal lives, has not abandoned us. His providential care sustains us moment by moment and we have the opportunity to respond to God's grace and to be a channel of it. We can, individually and collectively, shape world history so as to promote the kingdom of God.

History is ambiguous: stupid and wise, mean and kind, brutal and respectful. Like it or not, we are caught up in this swirl and our challenge is to "remember the marvels the Lord has done" (responsorial refrain, Ps 105:5a).

Meditation: What has been your experience of world history? What contribution have you made to world history in order to further the kingdom of God?

Prayer: Come, Holy Spirit, come. Give us the grace of wisdom to counter our stupidity; the grace of kindness to counter our meanness; the grace of respect to counter our brutality. Come, Holy Spirit, come.

Lostness: Looking for a Name

Readings: Mic 7:14-15, 18-20; Luke 15:1-3, 11-32

Scripture:
"But we must celebrate and rejoice,
  because your brother was dead and has come to life
      again;
  he was lost and has been found." (Luke 15:32)

Reflection: It was a brief conversation. A friend stated that we have a word for a spouse who loses a mate: widow/ widower. We have a word for a person who loses both parents: orphan. But we do not have a word for a parent who loses a child. True, we have a large lexicon describing a variety of feelings—grief, sorrow, terror, disbelief—but we do not have a word of identification for that grieving parent.

The father of the prodigal son lost his child, not to physical death but to that painful alienation that causes deep anxiety and hurt. Sin severed the family bond; repentance, along with compassion and forgiveness, restored it. This is the story of humanity. All of us have wandered to various degrees from one another and God. Thus we are always in the process of returning to our true country, the heart of God and to the human community. The proper response is one of rejoicing and celebration. Hopefully, the elder son eventually joined in.

Back for a moment to that missing word to describe a parent who loses a child. Do you have an answer?

No Name

We have a name, we do,
for a spouse who has lost a partner—
    widow/widower.
We have a name, we do,
for a child become parentless—
    orphan.
We do not have a name, we don't,
for parents who have lost a child.
So what shall it be?
Please write and tell me.

Meditation: When was the first time you experienced "lostness"? Describe an experience you have had of rejoicing and celebrating when something or someone was found.

Prayer: Kind and merciful God, we often stray far from you and one another. Give us the strength to foster that unity with you and union with one another that you desire. Teach us how to celebrate and rejoice whenever alienation and sin are conquered. We know that you delight in clemency and that you throw our sins into the bottom of the sea.

Good Old Human Nature or Jesus, the Psychologist

Readings: Exod 20:1-17; 1 Cor 1:22-25; John 2:13-25

Scripture:
But Jesus would not trust himself to them because he
    knew them all,
  and did not need anyone to testify about human nature.
He himself understood it well. (John 2:25)

Reflection: Christology is one of the most important areas of theology. Christologists attempt to say who Jesus is. And the answers are many: Jesus the Messiah; Jesus the Son of God; Jesus the Good Shepherd; Jesus the Bread of Life; Jesus the Healer. Pope Benedict XVI adds to this list Jesus the Philosopher, the one who teaches us the art of living and dying.

We might add yet another description of Jesus: Jesus the Psychologist. In John's gospel, we hear that no one needs to testify to Jesus about human nature because the Lord understands the human heart and its emotions. Jesus knows what makes us tick; he knows our motivations and our wishes, our foibles and our strengths. He is not a distant psychologist but one who draws close to us so that we might experience the Father's love and mercy.

When Jesus came to the temple in Jerusalem on the occasion of the Passover, that great moment of liberation for the

Israelites, he did a very dramatic thing. With a whip made out of cords he drove the cattle and money changers out of the temple. Not only was Jesus consumed with zeal for his Father's house, he also wanted to wake up the people to the reality that the Passover was a most sacred moment. More, he wanted the people to understand that God's liberating power extends even to the mystery of death.

If Jesus was a good psychologist, we witness this in spades as God gives the Decalogue to the Israelites through Moses. God, the divine psychologist, knew that we humans need guidelines and principles to keep our relationships in proper order. So the Ten Commandments were given that we might respect God and our fellow human beings. Good psychologists articulate the disciplines necessary for growth and development.

Psychologists who have wisdom and use power well are a true blessing to the human community. St. Paul saw in Jesus the power of God and the wisdom of God. More, it was in Jesus crucified that our divine psychologist taught us the supreme lesson of total self-giving. Anyone basing their psychology on such footing is blessed indeed.

Meditation: Which of the names of Jesus mentioned above do you find most fitting? In what sense is Jesus a good psychologist? What do you understand by "human nature"?

Prayer: Christ crucified, teach us again and again the wisdom of God. Help us to see that it is in total self-giving, and nowhere else, that we experience peace and joy.

Faith: An Endangered Species

Readings: 2 Kgs 5:1-15ab; Luke 4:24-30

Scripture:
Jesus said to the people in the synagogue at Nazareth:
. . . "Again, there were many lepers in Israel
  during the time of Elisha the prophet,
    yet not one of them was cleansed, but only Naaman the
      Syrian." (Luke 4:24a, 27)

Reflection: As a prophet, Jesus both teaches and heals. Following in the tradition of Elijah and Elisha, Jesus is about the furthering of the kingdom of God. In the synagogue in his hometown of Nazareth, Jesus' teaching is not accepted. More, his very life is threatened because he confronted the townspeople for failing to accept God's messenger. So many prophets forfeited their lives in doing the work of the Lord.

Elisha apparently had more success. Though Elisha was at first rejected, Naaman the army commander and leper followed Elisha's advice and plunged seven times into the Jordan. The miraculous healing turned Naaman into a believer: "Now I know that there is no God in all the earth, except in Israel" (2 Kgs 5:15b). Years later Jesus was standing on the banks of the Jordan and experienced the call to mission. The same God who healed Naaman also sent Jesus to bring truth and healing to a broken world.

During this season of Lent we ask for the grace to grow in our life of faith. In a culture of doubt and agnosticism, the atmosphere we breathe is hostile to religion. We reject not only the prophets of old but also anyone who claims to have the authority to speak the truth. Skepticism is rampant. Faith in God's wisdom and power is threatened on every side.

We need again and again to remind ourselves that the mysteries of our faith—creation, redemption, and sanctification—are ever present and manifest. God continues to give us life day by day, to heal our infirmities and weaknesses and sins, and to send the Holy Spirit into our hearts that we might grow in maturity and wisdom. We plunged into the baptismal waters seeking to be healed. We come to the altar of God to receive the Bread of Life. We celebrate the sacrament of reconciliation and are given the gift of peace.

Ralph Waldo Emerson wrote: "No man can predict when God will visit him, but he can leave the door open." Naaman left the door open and we know what happened.

Meditation: How has your faith grown over the years? Why are skepticism and agnosticism so strong in our culture? In what ways has God healed you?

Prayer: Lord God, grant us an increase of faith. You come to us every day to strengthen us and heal us. Our sins are many, our illnesses grave. Restore our health that we might serve you all the days of our life. Come, Lord Jesus, come.

God's Great Kindness and Mercy

Readings: Dan 3:25, 34-43; Matt 18:21-35

Scripture:
"And now we follow you with our whole heart,
  we fear you and we pray to you.
Do not let us be put to shame,
  but deal with us in your kindness and great mercy."
    (Dan 3:41-42)

Reflection: We simply cannot get away from it, the call to forgiveness and reconciliation. Given our human condition, everyone struggles with sinfulness, that proclivity we have to injure or even break relationships with God, with one another, with ourselves. We keep stepping on toes, even our own. So, we seek God's kindness and mercy lest we become discouraged or depressed.

We might question the degree of God's forgiveness. Is it offered more than once, let's say, two, three, even four times? As we look at our own history, we can assess how often we have forgiven those who hurt us, even how often we have forgiven ourselves. Well, Jesus wants to be absolutely clear: there is no end to God's mercy; it is as infinite as the ocean and the stars in the sky. Even seven times seventy times cannot exhaust God's gracious compassion.

But all this does invite presumption. Some might say: "Well, as long as God will forgive me, I don't have to work very hard on eradicating sin from my life." Such a disposition hardens our heart and the rain of God's mercy finds it difficult to permeate our being and bring about conversion. The offer of mercy and compassion demands sincere resolution if it is to be effective.

In Shakespeare's *Hamlet*, the king, Hamlet's uncle, has insight into sin and forgiveness: "My fault is past. But, o! what form of prayer / Can serve my turn? 'Forgiven me my foul murder?' / That cannot be since I am still possess'd / Of those effects for which I did the murder, / My crown, mine own ambition, and my queen" (3.3.51–55). Though God's mercy is boundless, our reception of it demands contrition.

Meditation: Do you struggle with self-forgiveness? Reflect on the times when you have been forgiven by God and by your family and friends. What counsel would you offer Hamlet's uncle regarding the effects of his sins?

Prayer: God of kindness and mercy, guide us out of the darkness of sin into the light of your grace. Help us to be compassionate toward those who hurt us; help us to be serious in our resolution not to sin again. We stand in need of your mercy and loving kindness.

Obedentia et Pax

Readings: Deut 4:1, 5-9; Matt 5:17-19

Scripture:
"Therefore, whoever breaks one of the least of these
   commandments
   and teaches others to do so
   will be called least in the Kingdom of heaven.
But whoever obeys and teaches these commandments
   will be called greatest in the Kingdom of heaven."
      (Matt 5:19)

Reflection: A key element in our life of discipleship is obedience. So significant is this that we speak of it in terms of life or death. God commands us to love (even our enemies), to forgive (without discrimination), and to be compassionate (to all). If we do so, we will live a fruitful spiritual life; if we do not, darkness will cover our minds and sickness will permeate our hearts.

Moses is strong and uncompromising in urging his people to observe God's statutes and decrees. He goes on to say that if they are obedient, this will give evidence that they are a wise and intelligent people. The challenge will be not to forget God's love for them but both to remember what God has done for them (liberation from slavery) and then to teach God's commandments and providence to their children.

The teaching of the commandments happens in two ways. First of all, by living out what God has instructed is to teach by obedience. Second, by giving verbal education, God's commandments are passed on to the next generation. We have here modeling and mentoring, witness and instruction. Every generation needs these two forms of formation.

In one of his essays John Henry Cardinal Newman wrote: "Our only safety lies in obedience; our only comfort in keeping it in view." In our modern culture there is a sense that by being obedient we lose our freedom. Such is not the case. It is precisely when we are obedient to what God asks, to our true nature, that we are truly free.

Pope John XXIII had as his episcopal motto: *Obedientia et Pax*—the path to peace lay through obedience. It is when our will is aligned to God's will that we experience that peace that the world cannot provide. And besides peace, there will also be a deep joy.

Meditation: What is your understanding of obedience? Is it a virtue that is freeing or enslaving? Is it possible to have peace and joy without obedience to God's word?

Prayer: God of peace and joy, open our ears to your word, open our hearts to your desires. Grant us the grace of obedience that Mary had in saying yes to the angel Gabriel. It is in that *fiat*, that "let it be done according to your will," that we will know the joy and peace of your presence.

Body Language

Readings: Jer 7:23-28; Luke 11:14-23

Scripture:
This is the nation that does not listen
to the voice of the LORD, its God,
or take correction.
Faithfulness has disappeared;
the word itself is banished from their speech. (Jer 7:28)

Reflection: Body language speaks volumes. Stiff necks, hard hearts, turning one's back—all things that communicate resistance and opposition. Jeremiah the prophet had to deal with a people who refused to walk in the ways of the Lord. Unwilling to take correction, unwilling to turn again to God in fidelity, they walked in darkness. The consequences of disunity, chaos, and violence became abiding elements in their history.

Body language also reveals whether we are with or against the Lord. Probably the telltale sign is the human eye. Jesus looked with compassion on the mute person and then he drove out the demon, enabling that person to speak. But there were people in the crowd whose eyes were hard, cynical, and testy. They did not see the goodness and healing power of Jesus. They were out to associate Jesus with the prince of demons, Beelzebul. Their seeing was followed by accusatory words.

One of the imperatives of Lent is fasting. Our Christian spirituality is aware of the tremendous importance of the body. If it is disciplined and ordered, our body will radiate and speak of peace. If not, it will become obvious to any attentive person that our house (our body) might fall into disrepair.

At the end of his poem "Tiger, Tiger," William Blake raises the question of whether God smiles at the innocent lamb, the same God who made the fierce tiger. The answer is in the affirmative. God smiles at the lamb, at the tiger, and at us. God is for us, not against us. God, revealed in Jesus, came among us so that we might regain our speech, be it verbal or of the body, so that we might find the unity and peace that are elements of the kingdom.

Meditation: How aware are you of your own and other's body language? What are some of the signs that we are with or against God? How important is a nod of the head, a pat on the back, a gracious smile?

Prayer: Healing Lord, enable us to speak the truth. May we treasure always the grace of language and use it for your glory. Fill our minds with holy thoughts; fill our language with words that convey your love and mercy. Come, Lord Jesus, come.

Wheat and Honey

Readings: Hos 14:2-10; Mark 12:28-34

Scripture:
"If only my people would hear me,
   and Israel walk in my ways,
I would feed them with the best of wheat,
   and with honey from the rock I would fill them."
         (Ps 81:13, 16)

Reflection: Two gifts of the Holy Spirit are wisdom and understanding. From the prophet Hosea we read, "Let him who is wise understand these things; / let him who is prudent know them" (Hos 14:9a), and from Mark's gospel, "And when Jesus saw that he answered with understanding, he said to him, 'You are not far from the Kingdom of God'" (Mark 12:34a).

The wheat of wisdom and the honey of understanding direct us to the paths of the Lord. Both gifts enlighten the mind to grasp the truth, the truth that sets us free. All of us struggle with ignorance; all of us struggle with misunderstanding. It is God's self-giving Spirit that empowers us to draw near to the kingdom.

So what is this wheat of wisdom? Aristotle, one of the greatest philosophers of all time, would have us believe that wise people have the ability to see the true value of things and to know what their purpose is. In light of today's gospel, wise people know the value of love, the greatest of all virtues, and they realize that it is this grace of love that leads to union with God and unity among people. The end is the kingdom of God, that reign in which God's providence rules and guides the human community. Just as wheat is the staple of the body, wisdom is the staple of the soul.

So what is this honey of understanding? Another philosopher and theologian by the name of Augustine wrote: *Nemo nisi per amicitiam congnoscitur* (You need to be a friend of a person before you understand that person). Understanding is more than an intellectual achievement. It also has an affective dimension. To understand God's word, the revelation coming from Scripture, we need to be in right relationship with the Lord. For years, St. Augustine could not embrace and accept Scripture because he lacked friendship with God. After his conversion and confession of sin, Augustine's understanding of divine things changed not only his own intellectual landscape but also the landscape of the western world. Augustine's writings were honey to so many people.

Meditation: In what sense is wisdom like wheat, understanding like honey? Who are the wisdom figures in your life? What have they taught you?

Prayer: Come, Holy Spirit, fill us with your wisdom, understanding, and love. Our minds are so limited, our hearts so narrow. Transform us through the wheat of your wisdom and the honey of your understanding. Come, Holy Spirit, come.

Striving to Know God

Readings: Hos 6:1-6; Luke 18:9-14

Scripture:
"Let us know, let us strive to know the LORD;
  as certain as the dawn is his coming,
  and his judgment shines forth like the light of day!
He will come to us like the rain,
  like spring rain that waters the earth." (Hos 6:3)

Reflection: What do we learn about God in the readings for today?

First of all, God desires love, not sacrifice or burnt offerings. Add to this the responsorial refrain: "It is mercy I desire, and not sacrifice" (Hos 6:6). Love and Mercy! St. Therese of Lisieux strove to know God, and, though she died before her twenty-fifth birthday, she came to the faith conviction that God was a God of love and mercy. This self-giving God revealed in Jesus is a God of total self-donation. And Jesus also revealed the compassion of God as he extended forgiveness to all. Since we are made in the image and likeness of God, our mission and our ministry is to be agents of love and mercy.

Second, God values the virtue of humility. The gospel story regarding the self-righteous Pharisee (who is not like the rest of sinful humanity) and the sinful tax collector ends with Jesus telling all of us that the prideful will be humbled and the humble will be exalted. Humility is living in the truth of things. And the truth is that all of us are sinners, be it the sin of greed, dishonesty, adultery, self-indulgence, anger, envy, or laziness. Our sins of commission and omission stare at us in the mirror. With eyes lowered, we beseech God's loving forgiveness.

Third, in striving to know our God whose coming is like the dawn and the rain, our God is gracious. We pray over the gifts of bread and wine: "Lord, by your grace you enable us to come to these mysteries with renewed lives." We come to know our God as a giver of all good gifts. Grace, this share in the very life of God, is constantly besieging us. Our task is to open our minds and hearts, to open our communities and nations, to this besieging love. Herein is our renewal; herein is our fullness of life.

How do we strive to know God? Surely in his works: creation, redemption, and sanctification. But also in our waking in the morning, in the gift of friendship, in the silence of midnight. And always God is a God of mercy, love, humility, and grace.

Meditation: How has your knowledge of God grown over the years? What role does revelation play in your coming to know God? Your personal experience?

Prayer: God of mystery, help us to come to know and love you. Deepen our faith and strengthen our reason. You are always present and our task is to be aware of your abiding love and mercy.

God's Light, Life, and Love

Readings: 2 Chr 36:14-16; 19-23; Eph 2:4-10; John 3:14-21

Scripture:
For God so loved the world that he gave his only Son,
　　so that everyone who believes in him might not perish
　　but might have eternal life. (John 3:16)

Reflection: Blessed Elizabeth of the Trinity (1880–1906) was a Carmelite nun from Dijon, France. It is reported that the last words she spoke were: "I am going to Light, to Life, to Love!" She died at age twenty-six.

John's gospel is filled with light, life, and love. Jesus is the Light of the world, the Bread of Life, and the manifestation of God's Love. In speaking to Nicodemus, Jesus was calling him to become an agent of light in a dark world. Darkness was needed for the wicked to conceal their guilt; the wicked hate the light. Nicodemus was called to be an agent of life. By sharing his faith in God's only son, Nicodemus would point people in the direction of eternal life. Nicodemus was called to be an agent of love, the extravagant love that God has for the world.

St. Paul, after his conversion, lived in the Light, Life, and Love of Jesus. This was his life of grace. This Apostle to the Gentiles is absolutely clear that all this was God's gift; none of it could be attributed to good works. When St. Paul did boast, and he was not hesitant to do so, it was always in the context of faith, faith in the richness of God's mercy.

Blessed Elizabeth of the Trinity is famous for the following prayer that might well transform our very lives: "O my God, Trinity whom I adore, help me to be utterly forgetful of self so as to be rooted in you, as changeless and calm as if I were already in eternity. May nothing disturb my peace or draw me out of you, my unchangeable One, but at every moment may I penetrate ever more deeply into the depth of your mysteries: Make me peaceful, make me your heaven, a home that you love and the place where you can be at rest; may I never leave you there alone, but be there entirely absorbed, in living faith, wholly adoring, freely given up to your creative action."

Meditation: How are you an agent of God's Light, Life, and Love? What does Blessed Elizabeth's prayer say to you?

Prayer: Blessed Trinity, may we praise your glory—your Light, Life, and Love. Grant us the grace and faith to believe that you truly dwell within us and that our souls are your heaven. May we respond today to your creative action within us.

Joseph's *Fiat*

Readings: 2 Sam 7:4-5a, 12-14a, 16; Rom 4:13, 16-18, 22; Matt 1:16, 18-21, 24a

Scripture:
Now this is how the birth of Jesus Christ came about.
When his mother Mary was betrothed to Joseph,
   but before they lived together,
  she was found with child through the Holy Spirit.
     (Matt 1:18)

Reflection: In preparing people for marriage, a form has to be filled out indicating one's freedom to enter into the sacrament of marriage. One might wonder what would have happened if Joseph had to deal with this process. Although Mary and Joseph were betrothed, she was pregnant. We know of God's intervention and how, through the obedience of both Joseph and Mary, salvation history would continue its course.

While realizing the importance of laws and forms and regulations, we also realize that the Holy Spirit often works in ways that transcend human order. What we celebrate on this feast of St. Joseph is the mystery of redemption and how Joseph played a significant role in God's plan to save humanity through the life, death, and resurrection of Jesus. That redemptive work would be done in conjunction with human agents and demand their cooperation. Mary's yes and Joseph's positive response to the divine dream were all part of God's loving design.

At bottom, this is a story about the birth of Jesus. True, Joseph was a righteous man and Mary was his loving mother, but it is Jesus who was the center of the story. Joseph and Mary would have it no other way. Much like John the Baptist's theme that he must decrease and Christ increase, the same is true of Joseph and Mary. Yet we must celebrate these parents of Jesus because of their proximity to the Savior of the world. It was precisely in that proximity that their greatness is to be found.

King David was promised an heir and a kingdom that would endure forever. That promise came to its full realization in Jesus whose coming inaugurated the kingdom that will never end. Today we celebrate the fact that Joseph played a major role in the fulfillment of God's faithful promise.

Meditation: In what lies greatness? What role does St. Joseph play in your life? Are dreams one way in which God speaks to you?

Prayer: St. Joseph, pray for us. Help us to discern the Lord's call in dreams, in the events of our life, in the beauty of creation, in the birth of a child. You were righteous and just. Intercede for us that we may emulate those virtues. Assist us in taking Mary into the home of our heart.

Our Mat

Readings: Ezek 47:1-9, 12; John 5:1-16

Scripture:
Jesus said to him [ill person], "Rise, take up your mat, and
    walk."
Immediately the man became well, took up his mat, and
    walked. (John 5:8-9)

Reflection: Paralysis and sickness come in many forms: intellectual, emotional, physical. A tiny germ can knock us down;
a word of rejection can spiral us into dejection; a loss of
energy by day's end leads to being brain-dead. But then the
refrain begins again and again: "Rise up!"

Our Christian call is to fullness of life, all the way into
eternal life. Jesus came to heal and restore us to health, to
share the very life of grace with us, to lead us in the way of
love, joy, and peace. The Lord himself has tasted our weari-
ness, our temptations, our being sick of heart at the death of
loved ones. And yet, day after day, Jesus arose to walk the
path the Father had marked out for him.

What was the mat that Jesus carried? Was it not our
"human condition," our innate poverty, our radical indi-
gence, our total dependency on the Father? The first Beati-
tude deals with the poor in spirit, for that is the universal
factor of all human life. As much as we try to cover up the

fact of our poverty, it keeps breaking through in our daily hunger, our need for air and water, our longing for intimacy and community. Our mat is essentially the same regardless of culture or time in history. Our mat is the gift and burden of human existence.

To be cured of a physical ailment is one thing; to be cured of our spiritual illness is another. It is during the season of Lent that we look deeply into our lives and ask the Lord to come and do radical surgery, excising those deep attitudes and values that are contrary to the Gospel. Again and again we hear the Ash Wednesday refrain: "Turn away from sin and believe in the gospel." But even this turning away is the work of the Lord. Our task is to respond to the grace of reconciliation.

The Russian author Fyodor Dostoevsky describes one form of illness as "a continual dissatisfaction, an inability to love anyone or anything, restlessness without an object, a disgust of the self." Only the words of Jesus can deal with these spiritual diseases. May we this day hear those glorious words: "Rise, take up your mat, and walk."

Meditation: How has the Lord cured you on your journey? What is the mat on which you lie? Is spiritual well-being a top priority in your life?

Prayer: Compassionate Jesus, continue to call us to fullness of life. Heal us of our narcissism and greed, of our anger and lust. May we rise up and do your work, the works of love and mercy. Come, Lord Jesus, come.

March 21: Wednesday of the Fourth Week of Lent

God's Work

Readings: Isa 49:8-15; John 5:17-30

Scripture:
Jesus answered the Jews:
"My father is at work until now, so I am at work."
(John 5:17)

Reflection: In her book *The Third Chapter: Passion, Risk, and Adventure in the 25 Years After 50,* Sara Lawrence-Lightfoot writes of a person who is too old to work and yet is too young to die. The accuracy of this statement depends on what we mean by work. As long as we are alive, we have work to do, if only the work of realizing more fully our humanity.

Jesus reminds us that his Father is always at work. The Divine Potter is always at the wheel shaping our individual lives and our world history. At times we are malleable and disposed to the divine touch. At other times, we are off doing our own thing and expressing no cooperation in furthering the kingdom. Wars attest to this as do all other activities that cause division and hurt. God's creative work never ceases, and, if we are truly silent, we can hear God's call to fullness of life and feel the divine touch of grace and mercy.

Isaiah was aware of God's work. God comforts his people and shows them his mercy. God makes highways level and cuts roads through mountains. God pities those who suffer and guides the thirsty to fresh water. God is active because God is love. God's love is analogous to a mother's affection, an affection and tenderness so deep that no child can be forgotten. We have a God who is gracious and merciful.

The documents of Vatican II refer to the Holy Spirit over 258 times. Listen carefully to how the council fathers describe the work of the Holy Spirit: makes the Gospel a reality, enables understanding, anticipates need, renews the church, sanctifies the people, builds up the Body of Christ, carries out the work of Christ. This is the Spirit that dwells in us through baptism and confirmation. As we journey through life, we do not travel alone. The Holy Spirit dwells within us helping us to see, love, and follow in the way of Christ.

As Jesus promised, we are not left orphans. God is present as our comforter, advocate, and defender through the gift of the Holy Spirit. A good Lenten practice is to pause upon retiring at night and recall our confirmation name as well as the words used in being signed with the oil of chrism: "_____, be sealed with the gift of the Holy Spirit." God's work continues day in and day out. *Deo gratias*.

Meditation: How do you emulate God's work? What role does the Holy Spirit play in your spirituality? Are you too old to work, yet too young to die?

Prayer: Spirit of the living God, continue to be our advocate, our defender, our comforter. Life's journey is long and trying. We need your wisdom and guidance, your courage and strength. Come, Holy Spirit, come.

Personal Faith: Sterile or Fruitful

Readings: Exod 32:7-14; John 5:31-47

Scripture:
"For if you had believed Moses,
    you would have believed me,
    because he wrote about me.
But if you do not believe his writings,
    how will you believe my words?" (John 5:46-47)

Reflection: Moses and Jesus had a difficult time. As they tried to communicate God's message to the people, the people were not properly disposed to receive it. Thus, rather than an obedient faith, Jesus and Moses encountered a stiff-necked people and much hardness of heart. Despite the resistance, Moses and Jesus challenged the people to turn from the darkness of sin and idolatry to the light of God's grace and mercy.

In a challenging theological work, *The Sacraments: The Word of God at the Mercy of the Body*, Louis-Marie Chauvet writes: "the self-*gift* God offers through the sacraments does not depend on the personal faith of the subjects: God gives freely through the power of the Spirit; but the fruitfulness of this gift in those who receive it, that is, the *reception* they give to this gift *as* grace, depends on their faith."

We all know of family situations in which parents express a deep and abiding love for their children. It sometimes happens that one or another of the children do not accept that love freely given. In fact, such a child, despite parental affection, becomes hostile and a deep alienation sets in. The love is there for the taking, but it must be embraced.

So too with the gift of faith. God's self-giving is universal, like the rays of the sun. But an individual or a nation can attempt to shield itself from the light and love of God. Our Lenten task is to offer a gracious hospitality to God's friendship and to live in accord with the divine will.

A footnote. Perhaps one reason that God's self-giving is not accepted is that the gift of faith is not for oneself alone. Once received, it must be shared. Thus, a serious responsibility is imposed on anyone who believes, and that responsibility is to share the good news of God's love revealed in Jesus. Authentic faith leads to evangelization.

Meditation: In what sense does faith depend on us? On your faith journey, what were two or three touchstone experiences? Confirmation? A success or failure? Reconciliation?

Prayer: Self-giving God, grant us the grace to embrace your friendship. Deepen our faith, our hope, and our love. Give us the wisdom to see your presence in the ordinary events of our life and then to share with others how you guide and direct us in your love. May your Holy Spirit fill our hearts this day.

Thinking Not Aright

Readings: Wis 2:1a, 12-22; John 7:1-2, 10, 25-30

Scripture:
The wicked said among themselves,
    thinking not aright:
"Let us beset the just one, because he is obnoxious to us;
    he sets himself against our doings." (Wis 2:1a, 12a)

Reflection: The word orthodoxy has fallen on hard times. To many it means a narrow dogmatism when in fact it means correct thinking, thinking aright about God and faith and life. Thoughts matter and once the mind becomes diseased, the heart and the hands do strange things. At the end of the first reading from the book of Wisdom we hear: "These were their thoughts, but they erred; / for their wickedness blinded them, / and they knew not the hidden counsels of God; / neither did they count on a recompense of holiness / nor discern the innocent souls' reward" (Wis 2:21-22).

Evil blinds the mind; evil prevents us from seeing the truth. Jesus, the light of the world, became the object of hatred for the leaders of Jerusalem. They sought to arrest and kill him. The leaders were ignorant of Jesus' origin and his true mission. More, threatened by the Lord's power to transform the minds and hearts of people, they wanted to eliminate him. We know the rest of the story.

Two things present themselves as a Lenten opportunity. First, we would do well to reflect and meditate deeply on who Christ is for us. By pondering John's gospel, by lifting our minds and hearts in prayer, by doing the works of mercy, we participate in the life of Jesus and come to know him more intimately. We realize again that he came from the Father and that his mission is one of reconciling all of creation back to the Father. We come to know that Jesus is the way, the truth, and the life. If we think aright, we will experience God's love and mercy in Jesus.

Second, we need the courage and humility to face our own wickedness and evil. By facing our sin, the ways in which we hurt others and weaken and break relationships, we get in touch with the dark side of our being. Thinking aright here is terribly important. That ancient refrain, "Lord Jesus, have mercy on us, for we are sinners," is a powerful Lenten prayer. By facing the truth, Jesus sets us free through divine mercy and forgiveness.

Meditation: Why is thinking aright so important? How has your knowledge of Jesus grown in the last five years? What evil lurks in your heart?

Prayer: Lord Jesus, grant us the gifts of wisdom and understanding. Help us to see you in the breaking of bread and in the suffering of our neighbor. Help us to realize that we are saints and sinners, capable of so much good and so much evil. Set us free through the gift of your Holy Spirit.

March 24: Saturday of the Fourth Week of Lent

The Soul's Greatest Happiness

Readings: Jer 11:18-20; John 7:40-53

Scripture:
Some in the crowd who heard these words of Jesus said,
    "This is truly the Prophet."
Others said, "This is the Christ."
But others said, "The Christ will not come from Galilee,
    will he?" (John 7:40-41)

Reflection: Hans Urs von Balthasar (1905–1988), one of the great theologians of the twentieth century, talked about happiness and what was the soul's supreme bliss. His answer was direct and clear. The soul's greatest joy is giving back to God what God has given to the soul. Happiness lies in the "reciprocity of giving."

So what has God given us? The answer: God's very self! Before we look at the gifts of time, talent, and treasure, before we enumerate the gifts of freedom, family, and friends, we receive uncreated grace, God's very life. This gift comes to us in Jesus, the prophet, the Christ, the savior of the world. Our task and our happiness lie in returning the gift to God by sharing Christ, God's mercy and love, with everyone we meet. When this is done in faith, happiness, and joy, then peace will enter our souls.

We return again and again to the ancient paradox of dying and rising. Be it the grain of wheat, the acorn, the caterpillar, unless there is a death no new life is forthcoming. At the heart of Lent is the paschal mystery, Jesus' self-donation for the life of the world. As we prepare for the Easter mysteries, we are called upon to participate in the Lord's joys and sorrows, in his mission and ministry. It's all about discipleship.

Giving is a mark of love. God's love for us comes first. What we do with love determines both our character and our destiny. By returning that love to God by serving others we conform ourselves to the likeness God has implanted in us. Failure to enter into that process of receiving and giving spells tragedy.

Fr. Ladislaus Boros used the expression "unnoticed Giving" to describe how the human person resembles God's generosity. No blowing of trumpets, no seeking applause, no drawing attention to oneself—rather, the simple, steady being for others in a life of selflessness. And if this requires the cross, so be it.

Meditation: What has been your experience of happiness? Is generosity different from love? What are some of the blessings God has given you and what have you done with those graces?

Prayer: Generous and loving God, all life, all holiness, all good things come from you. May we receive these gifts with gratitude; may we then share these gifts with those in need. Give us a generous heart. Help us to make Jesus present and manifest in our days.

March 25: Fifth Sunday of Lent

This Hour

Readings: Jer 31:31-34; Heb 5:7-9; John 12:20-33

Scripture:
"The hour has come for the Son of Man to be glorified.
Amen, amen, I say to you,
   unless a grain of wheat falls to the ground and dies,
   it remains just a grain of wheat;
   but if it dies, it produces much fruit." (John 12:23b-24)

Reflection: In Shakespeare's *Hamlet* we hear: "The time is out of joint; O cursed spite, / That ever I was born to set it right!" (1.5.188–89). Jesus would have a different refrain: "Time is out of joint, indeed, and the Father has sent me to set it right."

The reason Jesus came was to redeem the world, and he would do that mission in accord with the Father's time and the Father's design. The hour had come and Jesus would not back away from it. The design was one of total sacrificial love, and Jesus would embrace that cross in loving obedience.

In his *Introduction to the Devout Life*, St. Francis de Sales, being the good psychologist that he was (as well as a Doctor of the Church, which he is), reminds us that our relationship with time can be somewhat mixed up: "We are often in the condition of those who long for fresh cherries in autumn and for fresh grapes in spring." This is not unusual. The great

Augustine asked for chastity, but not yet; Jesus talks about those who dance when they should mourn, and those who grieve when they should rejoice. Wisdom and obedience are both necessary if we are to live in accord with God's time and design.

The hour comes for the grain of wheat to fall to the ground, die unto itself, and yield a rich harvest. The hour comes when the grapes are thrown into the vat on their way to becoming wine. The hour comes for God's glory—God's light and love and life—to be made manifest to a world in need of salvation.

Each of us is called to be sensitive to "the hour" in which God will ask us to lay down our life for others. In the paradox of dying and rising, we reveal God's glory and manifest God's beauty. And we can be assured that when the time comes, the grace will also be at hand.

In Goethe's *Faust* we hear echoes of the gospel passage for today: "Nothing but time can give the brew its strength." We might paraphrase: nothing but graced obedience reveals the glory of God.

Meditation: How do you know when your hour is at hand? What is your relationship to time—to the past, the present, and the future?

Prayer: Lord Jesus, help us to embrace your Father's time and design. When the call is heard, may we respond immediately. Be with us in our hour.

God Our Emmanuel

Readings: Isa 7:10-14; 8:10; Heb 10:4-10; Luke 1:26-38

Scripture:
The angel Gabriel was sent from God
  to a town of Galilee called Nazareth,
  to a virgin betrothed to a man named Joseph,
  of the house of David,
  and the virgin's name was Mary. (Luke 1:26-27)

Reflection: There is so much information in this single verse of Scripture. God has a plan; there are creatures known as angels; our attention is directed to a small town in the Middle East; a wedding is about to take place between Joseph and Mary; the fiancé is of royal lineage. And that is just the start of the story, a story that will forever change history.

Like Moses before the burning bush, we are on sacred ground. This is not just a story of a past event; this is a story about our own existence. We are included in Mary's yes; we are the reason why God breaks into history in a unique way; we are called, like Joseph and Mary, to participate in salvation history. Just as Mary was troubled and wanting in knowledge, we too struggle to wrap our arms around God's mysterious ways.

Before Gabriel was sent to Mary, God was laying the foundation of his plan through the prophet Isaiah. We read: "Therefore the Lord himself will give you this sign: / the virgin shall be with child, and bear a son, / and shall name him Emmanuel, / which means 'God is with us!'" (Isa 7:14; 8:10)

As we approach the Easter mystery of the Lord's resurrection, our faith proclaims that God is with us in all dimensions of human existence. God is Emmanuel when we are born or get ill, when we commit ourselves to marriage or holy orders, when we need forgiveness or the strengthening of the Holy Spirit, when we need daily and weekly nourishment. God is faithful to us in all our joys and sorrows.

Mary is there too. From her place in God's kingdom, she continues to intercede for us as we struggle to respond to God's initiatives. We are asked, like her, to have an obedient faith and to conceive within our souls the word of God. The mystery of the annunciation has an eternal element to it. Angels and other messengers are continuously being sent to invite us to participate in the great paschal mystery. When we give our yes as Mary did, we experience a peace and joy that knows no end.

Meditation: What role does Mary play in your spirituality? In what ways is God manifest in your daily life? Who are the angels and messengers in your life who call you to deeper discipleship?

Prayer: Mary, mother of Jesus and of the church, continue to intercede for us. We need the grace to hear God's call and the courage to respond as you did to what God asks. Be with us on this perilous journey.

Fidelity: Active and Passive

Readings: Num 21:4-9; John 8:21-30

Scripture:
So Jesus said to them . . .
"The one who sent me is with me.
He has not left me alone,
   because I always do what is pleasing to him."
      (John 8:28a, 29)

Reflection: In Aelred Squire's excellent book *Asking the Fathers*, he speaks of our common vocation in terms of responding to the fullness of God's presence in our everyday life. Every person, event, and circumstance challenges us to discern God's work and then to make an appropriate response. Squire speaks to two fidelities: active and passive. Active fidelity involves doing our duties and fulfilling the obligations of our chosen state in life. Passive fidelity is lived when we say yes to what God sends our way, be it suffering or joy.

Jesus did what was pleasing to the Father. The Lord's mission was about bringing the kingdom of God into the world. Jesus did this by his preaching, teaching, healing, and compassionate ministries. Jesus' fidelity was truly active. We witness this in the Sermon on the Mount, in the healing of the paralytic, in the calling of the Twelve. Jesus was busy about many things.

But there was also that graced, passive fidelity. Jesus endured the agony in the garden, the crowning of thorns, the crucifixion. Jesus suffered at every level of existence: physical, psychological, and spiritual. He did the Father's will as much by what he endured as by what he did. Our discipleship involves both types of fidelity.

In Joseph Conrad's story *Youth* we read: "I thought it fine; the fidelity of the old ship was fine." We know that envy is a sin, but what a temptation here not to be jealous of the old ship that did its duty year in and year out. Would that in our eulogy we might hear a friend proclaim about us: "I thought it fine; the fidelity of _____ was fine."

On this long Christian journey we will have to struggle with getting tired, even with giving up. That is why we need the example of Jesus and the witness of the saints who help us to persevere, come what may. Fidelity, whether active or passive, is possible because of the gift of the Holy Spirit.

Meditation: What is your understanding of active and passive fidelity? Who are the faithful people in your life? What do you do when you become weary of either trying to do good or enduring the sufferings of life?

Prayer: Come, Holy Spirit, come. Strengthen us to be faithful to what God asks of us and to what God allows to happen in our lives. We are weak and in need of your courage. May we be like a fine old ship that models great fidelity.

The Slavery of Sin

Readings: Dan 3:14-20, 91-92, 95; John 8:31-42

Scripture:
Jesus answered them, "Amen, amen, I say to you,
 everyone who commits sin is a slave to sin." (John 8:34)

Reflection: As we draw near to Holy Week and to the liberating events of our faith—the conquering of sin on Good Friday and the conquering of death on Easter Sunday—we do well to pause and reflect again on what sin does in our lives. Essentially, it darkens the intellect, preventing our seeing the truth, and it weakens the will, thereby blocking a graced use of our freedom.

Slavery comes in many forms. Physically, people have been sold into slavery and their freedom denied. Also at the physical level is enslavement to tobacco and alcohol and other forms of drugs. Psychologically, one can become a slave to a poor self-image or to anxieties that fill the heart with terror. Morally, an immoral lifestyle can erode the proper functioning of freedom. And spiritually, when one turns away from God, we walk into the darkness of sin and lose our way.

Jesus came to set us free and to bring us the fullness of life. When sin, by contrast, enters the soul, our freedom and peace are diminished and can even vanish. The struggle between grace and sin allows no exemptions. Every individual, every family and friendship, every community and nation, faces the tension between light and darkness, love and hate, life and death. In setting before his people the choice of life or death, Moses begged them to choose life.

Darkness and Weakness! When truth is obscured by the lie and freedom is impeded by immorality, we must invoke the Holy Spirit to come and enlighten us to see and to enkindle within us the strength of God's power. It is the saving power of the Spirit of Jesus that restores us to friendship with God.

Jesus is the light of the world guiding us to truth. The Holy Spirit is God's great gift to us, a gift that strengthens and fortifies us on our pilgrim journey. We never travel alone.

Meditation: What are the consequences of sin in your life? Have you ever felt like a slave, unable to discern and make good choices? How important is the sacrament of reconciliation in your spiritual life?

Prayer: Lord Jesus, enlighten our minds and send your Spirit to fortify our hearts. Too easily we yield to temptation and plunge into darkness and weakness. Without your loving presence, we end up as slaves to our passions. Come, Lord Jesus, and set us free.

Covenant: God's Gift of Friendship

Readings: Gen 17:3-9; John 8:51-59

Scripture:
When Abram prostrated himself, God spoke to him: . . .
"I will maintain my covenant with you
    and your descendants after you
    throughout the ages as an everlasting pact,
    to be your God and the God of your descendants after
        you." (Gen 17:3, 7)

Reflection: At the center of our faith life is that relationship we call covenant, a mutual, reciprocal bonding between God and humankind. God is not only creator. God not only gives life but, through knowledge and love of us, binds us to himself. That gift of friendship is what St. Thomas Aquinas calls grace (*amacitia Dei*). God established that friendship with Abram (Abraham), with his offspring, with all of humanity through the coming of Jesus.

But that covenant/friendship faced obstacles. In the gospel today Jesus faced the hostility of some of Abraham's offspring who refused to accept the prophetic ministry of Jesus. They were unable to understand Jesus' relationship with both God the Father and their own father Abraham. Jesus' offer of a new covenant fell on barren soil.

In our Western culture, characterized so often by a radical individualism, the concepts of covenant and friendship have fallen on hard times. In the United States well over 40 percent of marriages (covenant and friendship agreements) end in divorce. Every year more and more people do not practice their faith, failing to return to God a portion of their time in worship. But God is faithful even though we may not be. God continues to offer the gift of friendship to anyone who has a modicum of faith.

But there is more here than individualism and various degrees of narcissism. Friendships and covenant relationships are very demanding, for they involve in a deep way our freedom, our personal will. Because of friendship's intrinsic elements of mutuality and reciprocity, both parties in such relationships have to be willing to compromise and sacrifice. It is precisely here that so many walk away, heading down that path of radical isolation and loneliness. No wonder our psychologists and psychiatrists are so busy.

Meditation: What is your understanding of covenant and friendship? Who is your best friend and what does that friendship involve?

Prayer: God of Abraham, Father of Jesus, deepen our faith in your gift of friendship. Help us to treasure above all things your life within us. May we be faithful covenant partners with you; may we share your friendship with others.

Sacred Places and Stories

Readings: Jer 20:10-13; John 10:31-42

Scripture:
He [Jesus] went back across the Jordan
   to the place where John first baptized, and there he
      remained. (John 10:40)

Reflection: In his excellent book *Landscapes of the Sacred: Geography and Narrative in American Spirituality*, Professor Belden Lane demonstrates the importance of place and story in various spiritual traditions. Geography played a big role in the life of Jesus. More specifically, the Jordan River was the site where our Lord began his public ministry in being baptized by John the Baptist. It is no surprise that Jesus would return time and time again to that sacred landscape to refresh his spirit and renew his commitment.

It was at the Jordan that God called Jesus his beloved son. It was at Caesarea Philippi that Peter would acknowledge Jesus as the Messiah. It was in the Upper Room that Jesus instituted the Eucharist. And it was on Mount Calvary that our redemption was won for us. Sacred places all, and each one has a unique and powerful story.

C. S. Lewis claimed that some stories get under our skin and cannot be gotten rid of. The story of Jesus is one of those transforming narratives. For two thousand years that story has been told in all of our liturgical seasons. We are taken back to Bethlehem, Nazareth, Cana of Galilee, Jericho, and Mount Tabor where we observe the marvelous works of God. If we stop and ponder these moments and appropriate their meaning, our lives will be changed. The story will get under our skin and will not leave us.

In Thomas Hardy's *The Return of the Native* we read: "Such a rare plant in such a wild place it grieves me to see." Jesus was a rare plant, indeed, the Son of God. Jesus came to a wild place, our planet Earth to take on our humanity. And the story that unfolds should cause grief in the heart of humanity. For here was Love come to reconcile all creation to the Father. Here was Life that was given for our salvation. Here was the Light of the world and sent to show us the way. What grief untold we have here as the Love, Life, and Light was rejected.

Geography and narrative, place and story, space and time. This is our human condition and it is in this environment that we live and move and have our being. And, as Pierre Teilhard de Chardin would remind us, we truly live in the divine milieu.

Meditation: What is the most important place in your life? Where do you go to be renewed and refreshed? To whom have you told your story?

Prayer: God of space and time, give us an appreciation of our sacred landscapes. Be they a river or a forest, a home or a village, a mountain or a valley, help us to see the spiritual fullness of that sacred geography. Help us to understand the story of Jesus.

March 31: Saturday of the Fifth Week of Lent

Looking for Jesus

Readings: Ezek 37:21-28; John 11:45-56

Scripture:
Now the Passover of the Jews was near,
    and many went up from the country to Jerusalem
    before Passover to purify themselves.
They looked for Jesus. (John 11:55-56a)

Reflection: All of us are searchers and seekers. We are looking for that "something" or "someone"—a relationship, a value, an achievement—that will satisfy the hungers of the heart and soul. For some, fulfillment is sought in fame; for others, in the accumulation of possessions or the acquisition of power. Deep down we know that we are made for relationships, being connected with our God, with one another, indeed, with ourselves. It is through the grace of love that we experience union and unity, the intimacy that alone overflows into peace and joy.

As we approach Holy Week we see people looking for Jesus for a variety of reasons. The Pharisees sought Jesus; the Romans sought Jesus; the disciples sought Jesus. The motivations ranged from destruction to a deeper friendship. It would appear as if Jesus is almost in the passive voice here but such is not the case. Jesus is in the active voice, for he is the one who is seeking the well-being of the Pharisees, the Romans, and his disciples.

A basic principle in the spiritual realm, one that is frequently forgotten or not even recognized, is that before we seek God, God is always seeking us. God is that famous "Hound of Heaven" described by Francis Thompson. God pursues us "down the nights and down the days." Was it not Jesus who came down to us in the mystery of the incarnation, seeking us out, to reconcile all of us and all creation to the Father?

Perhaps the psalmist has the secret, not about seeking, but about being found. In Psalm 46:11 we read: "Be still and confess that I am God." Rather than fleeing down the nights and days of history, rather than reading yet another spiritual book, rather than getting caught in an activist life of only doing good deeds, we need but be still and await the invasion of grace, God's love and life pouring into our soul like the morning sun or the spring rain. Maybe all we have to do is stop and let the "Hound of Heaven" find our hiding place.

Meditation: Where do you look for Jesus? Why is it so hard to sit still and rest in the presence of God? What are your hiding places?

Prayer: Lord Jesus, we do look for you and we do find you in the eyes of the poor, in the cry of the suffering. But we know that as much as we seek you, you are the principal agent of our longings. You seek us day in and day out. Help us to be still; help us to be found.

The Transforming Power of Redemption

Readings: Isa 50:4-7; Phil 2:6-11; Mark 14:1–15:47

Scripture:
And immediately a cock crowed a second time.
Then Peter remembered the words that Jesus had said to
    him,
  "Before the cock crows twice you will deny me three
      times."
He broke down and wept. (Mark 14:72)

Reflection: In meditating on the passion of our Lord, we
witness the Lord's suffering at various levels. There is the
agonizing torture of the crowning with thorns and the ex-
treme physical pain of the crucifixion. Then there is the psychological torment of betrayal, both by Judas and by Peter.
The one selling his Master for money and the other maintain-
ing that he never knew the man. Add to this the incredible
experience of seeming spiritual abandonment—"My God,
my God, why have you abandoned me?" (Ps. 22:2a)—and
we wonder if anything could be worse.

But the focus of faith must not remain just at the level of
suffering, be it physical, psychological, or spiritual. Our faith
draws us into the mystery of redemption, for it is precisely
through Jesus' obedience to the cross that our salvation is
won. It is here that death and sin are conquered, once for all.

Thus, our meditation on the passion must culminate in profound gratitude that our God loves us so much. Our contemplation of this mystery must also elicit from our hearts deep sorrow for our part in the Lord's anguish, through personal and communal sin.

In the devotion of the Stations of the Cross, we move from one scene to another with the refrain: "We adore you, O Christ, and we praise you. Because by your holy cross you have redeemed the world." Redemption is about the reestablishment of unity and order. What was broken, has now been fixed; what was disordered and chaotic, is now mended and made whole. In faith we proclaim that we know that our redeemer lives.

In *Mere Christianity*, C. S. Lewis reminds us that redemption is not mere improvement but rather something much deeper: "God became man to turn creatures into sons: not simply to produce better men of the old kind but to produce a new kind of man." On this Passion Sunday we rejoice in the fact that, through the mystery of the cross, we are new creatures, daughters and sons of our creative, redeeming, loving God.

Meditation: What do you understand by redemption? In what ways do you participate in the sufferings of Jesus: physically, psychologically, and spiritually?

Prayer: Crucified Lord, give us the grace to kneel before the cross and adore you. Help us to understand the extravagance of your love and the horror of sin. As we celebrate Palm Sunday, may we do so with deep reverence and awe.

April 2: Monday of Holy Week

The Fragrance of the Oil

Readings: Isa 42:1-7; John 12:1-11

Scripture:
Mary took a liter of costly perfumed oil
 made from genuine aromatic nard
 and anointed the feet of Jesus and dried them with her
  hair;
 the house was filled with the fragrance of the oil.
  (John 12:3)

Reflection: Just as Mary anointed the feet of Jesus, the Lord continues to come to us in the sacrament of the sick. When sickness is upon us or death is near, a priest is called to administer God's loving concern. Again we realize how complete the incarnation is: Jesus was obedient unto death and the administration of Mary must have been a great source of consolation to him.

The fragrance of the oil was tainted, however, by two factors: the betrayal of Judas and the plan of the chief priests to kill both Jesus and Lazarus. In the air was the odor of hatred and deception. Judas was a thief; the chief priests violated their calling. A short time later Jesus would be at another meal, the Last Supper, and would again have to deal with the forces of evil.

The Jesuit theologian Gerald O'Collins, in his work *A Biblical, Historical and Systematic Study of Jesus*, tells of four evils that are part of our human condition, evils that Jesus came to save us from: alienation, death, ignorance, and absence of good. It is from these evils that we pray to be delivered in the Our Father. In our gospel passage today we see alienation as Judas separates himself from the community; we witness death in the plotting of the chief priests; then there is sheer ignorance and absence of good as we watch Judas the Iscariot steal from the contributions and stumble toward his demise.

Jesus confronts these evils still in coming to us sacramentally. It is in the sacrament of reconciliation that we hear the words of forgiveness; it is in the Eucharist, at the penitential rite, that we beg for God's mercy; it is in the sacrament of the sick that the Lord scatters the darkness of death and promises us everlasting life.

Yes, we do always have the poor with us. And yes, we always have the Lord Jesus, and if we are sensitive, we will be able to smell the aroma of grace.

Meditation: Which of the four evils do you struggle with the most? When do you sense the presence of God's grace? In praying the Our Father, focus on the phrase, "deliver us from evil."

Prayer: Lord Jesus, you who were obedient unto death, deliver us from the evils within and around us. May the fragrance of your sacrament refresh and sustain us. May we always be thankful for your loving presence.

Night and the Cock's Crow

Readings: Isa 49:1-6; John 13:21-33, 36-38

Scripture:
Reclining at table with his disciples, Jesus was deeply
    troubled and testified,
  "Amen, amen, I say to you, one of you will betray me."
      (John 13:21)

Reflection: One does not want to see their name on this list: Judas, Marcus Junius Brutus, Benedict Arnold—traitors all. For a variety of reasons—greed, revenge, spite—they betrayed a relationship and did great harm to others and eventually to themselves. Satan entered their souls and brought about darkness and death.

In the case of Judas, the betrayal was particularly heinous because he was specially chosen and mentored by Jesus. They shared in the work of the kingdom; they traveled together with the other disciples; and, they broke bread together at a common table. The crimes of Brutus and Benedict Arnold were of a different nature. These traitors were not in the intimate company of their victims. And then Judas used the kiss to complete his act of treachery.

"Jesus was deeply troubled." Not only was Judas planning to turn Jesus over, but Peter would also become a source of sorrow for the Lord. Though boastful about his claim to fidelity, Peter would also deny the Lord while the other disciples, except John, would hightail it away from danger. Jesus was troubled over their cowardice and what would be the fallout from their running away.

There are two images in our gospel passage that might haunt us. The first is that frightful phrase: "And it was night" (John 13:30b). We read that Judas took the morsel at the meal and left. This was more than the dark night of the soul; this was the dark night of sin at its worst. Judas walked away from the Light into the darkness of death.

The other phrase: "the cock will not crow before you deny me three times" (John 13:38b). For many Christians, when the sound of the cock crowing is heard, one's imagination immediately goes back to the exchange between Peter and Jesus. Before dawn would come, Peter would utter his three-fold denial. No wonder, then, that Jesus' soul was troubled.

Meditation: Why is our personal sin a betrayal of God? Do the images of "night" and the "cock's crow" influence your spirituality? When is your soul troubled?

Prayer: Jesus, you are faithful to us even when we deny you by the way we live. Draw us out of the night into your light. Give us the grace to be faithful to the friendship you offer us. Heal us of our cowardice.

April 4: Wednesday of Holy Week

Quenching the Thirst of Jesus

Readings: Isa 50:4-9a; Matt 26:14-25

Scripture:
The Lord GOD is my help,
    therefore I am not disgraced;
I have set my face like flint,
    knowing that I shall not be put to shame.
He is near who upholds my right. (Isa 50:7-8a)

Reflection: As we venture more deeply into Holy Week and approach the passion of the Lord, we have to ask: "How did Jesus do it?" Not only will the Lord have to suffer the agony of the crucifixion, he also has to endure the betrayal of friends and the hostility of the very people he came to save. In his obedience to the Father's will, his strength would come from his intimacy with the Father and in the power of the Holy Spirit.

Isaiah the prophet gives us an insight into who God is and how God works. God is our helper; God is always near at hand; God will not allow us to be disgraced. The psalmist as well offers the same message: "The LORD is my shepherd; / there is nothing I lack" (Ps 23:1). The God who creates, knows, and loves us is also the God who gives us the courage and strength to complete our mission.

Jesus came to shoulder the burden of sins and to lead us through death into the glory of the resurrection. He took upon himself the sin of Judas, the sin of Peter, and our sins. In offering his life for the salvation of the world he has set us free and has offered us the gift of hope. God gave his Son more than just a "well-trained tongue"; God gave Jesus the power and the wisdom to redeem the world.

In asking how did Jesus do what he did, we might also ask how did Blessed Mother Teresa of Calcutta do what she did? Surely one source of her strength and courage could be found in her identification with "the mystery of the thirst of Jesus Crucified," as she wrote in one of her letters. And this thirst was not just in her meditation on the historical Jesus on Calvary; it was the thirst and agony of the poor people of Calcutta and around the world. Mother Teresa committed her life and the life of her sisters to quenching that thirst as much as possible. What she did was rooted in the deep spirituality of being identified with Jesus. The Lord was her helper and she was a loving agent of God's compassion.

Meditation: In what ways has God been your helper? Wherein lies your strength to do good and endure suffering? In meditating on the crucifixion, does the image of the thirst of Jesus move you to action?

Prayer: Lord Jesus, deepen our faith in the Father's presence in our lives. May we emulate Mother Teresa in quenching your thirst by being for others. Strengthen us for the journey for we are weak and often weary.

The Eternal Season of Love

Readings: Exod 12:1-8, 11-14; 1 Cor 11:23-26; John 13:1-15

Scripture:
Before the feast of Passover, Jesus knew that his hour had
   come
  to pass from this world to the Father.
He loved his own in the world and he loved them to the
   end. (John 13:1)

Reflection: The famous passage from the book of Ecclesiastes
holds so much truth: "There is an appointed time for everything, / and a time for every affair under the heavens" (3:1).
There is a season to come and to leave; a season to change
water into wine and to suffer the agony in the garden; a time
to be baptized and a time to have a final meal with one's
friends. Jesus knew that the hour was upon him to return to
the Father, his mission accomplished.

But whatever the season, the keynote was that of love.
Jesus cured the paralytic out of love; he called the disciples
out of love; he protected the woman caught in adultery out
of love; he proclaimed the kingdom of God out of love; he
instituted the Eucharist out of love. Right to the end, it was
love that defined his mission and his person.

Just to be clear, Jesus took a towel and basin and washed
the feet of the disciples. In his simple yet powerful act, his

love took on flesh in a unique way. Love must be expressed in service, in being "for" others in the humblest of tasks. All the great saints in the church would emulate his gesture and reach out to those in need. The washing of feet also finds expression in living out the spiritual and corporal works of mercy: feeding the hungry, giving drink to the thirsty, clothing the naked . . . We wash the feet of others by instructing the ignorant, extending forgiveness, praying for the living and the dead . . . Our Christian lives begin in love at our baptism and end in love as we return to the God who created us.

St. Paul gives us a beautiful summary of the season of love: "I received from the Lord what I also handed on to you, that the Lord Jesus, on the night he was handed over, took bread, and, after he had given thanks, broke it and said, 'This is my body that is for you. Do this in remembrance of me'" (1 Cor 11:23-24). Here is the season of total self-giving; here is the season of our redemption.

Meditation: What have been the greatest seasons of your life? Was the grace of love at the center of those moments? What is your understanding of the Eucharist? How has that understanding grown over the years and seasons of your life?

Prayer: Jesus, your love is eternal. You came to us out of love and you loved us to the end. Now, this day, you plead for us at the right hand of the Father. Give us the wisdom to understand your love and the grace to live it.

Awesome: What Jesus Did For Us

Readings: Isa 52:13–53:12; Heb 4:14-16; 5:7-9;
John 18:1–19:42

Scripture:
After this, aware that everything was now finished,
   in order that the Scripture might be fulfilled,
     Jesus said, "I thirst." (John 19:28)

Reflection: It was after praying the Stations of the Cross
(watching Jesus be condemned, falling three times, being
nailed to the cross, dying) that a small third grader ap-
proached his pastor and said. "You know, Father, if you stop
to think about it, what Jesus did for us was awesome." The
pastor told me that this was the best Good Friday homily
that could have been written.

What Jesus did for us was filled with awe: coming into
history in the incarnation; healing so many who suffered
from sickness and sin; calling people to follow in this way;
telling stories and proclaiming God's love; suffering and
dying and rising that we might be saved. Too often we do
not pause to think well and thoroughly on what Jesus did
and continues to do for us.

Here is a poem I sent to the insightful and faith-filled third
grader:

Awesome

But you have to stop,
then you have to think,
and then let the heart take over.
If you do,
something "awesome" strikes the soul.

But we are in a hurry,
our thinking is superficial,
our hearts so often hardened—
the result: the soul is not touched.

It takes a third grader,
a nascent philosopher,
to set the example
to teach us how to live.

Mediation: How often do you pause and think about what God has done for you? What devotions keep you in daily and weekly contact with God? What fills you with awe?

Prayer: Lord Jesus, thank you for all you do for us. Let us never take your friendship for granted. Fill us with the gift of reverence and awe that we might praise your Father and be open to the gift of the Holy Spirit. "We adore you, O Christ, and we praise you, because by your Holy Cross you have redeemed the world."

Amazed!

Readings: Gen 1:1–2:2 or 1:1, 26-31a; Gen 22:1-18 or 22:1-2, 9a, 10-13, 15-18; Exod 14:15–15:1; Isa 54:5-14; Isa 55:1-11; Bar 3:9-15, 32–4:4; Ezek 36:16-17a, 18-28; Rom 6:3-11; Mark 16:1-7

Scripture:
He [young man] said to them, "Do not be amazed!
You seek Jesus of Nazareth, the crucified.
He has been raised; he is not here.
Behold the place where they laid him." (Mark 16:6)

Reflection: The Easter fire, the Easter candle, the Easter water, the Easter Scriptures—alleluia, alleluia, alleluia! How can we not be amazed at the glory of God revealed in the mystery of the resurrection? He who was dead is alive! He who was crucified is now victorious! He who was plunged in sorrow restores joy to the world!

How can we not be amazed as the Exsultet is sung and we hear about that happy fault, that necessary sin of Adam? How can we not be amazed at how Jesus broke the prison-bars of death and scattered the darkness of night? How can we not be amazed at how innocence is restored and mourners now rejoice? Our hearts are filled with joy as we hear sung: "May this flame be found still burning by the Morning Star: the one Morning Star who never sets, Christ your Son, who, coming back from death's domain, has shed his peaceful light on humanity, and lives and reigns for ever and ever."

St. Paul continues our amazement as he reminds us that our old, sinful self has been crucified with Jesus and that we now live a whole new life in him. Sin and death have been vanquished. All this is grounded in our baptism wherein we are given the gift of new life. St. Paul is speaking from experience. The risen Lord freed him from the slavery of sin and called him to proclaim Christ crucified, Christ risen. This Apostle to the Gentiles participated deeply in the great paschal mystery of the life, death, and resurrection of Jesus.

Another dimension of amazement in our Easter Vigil is our celebrating this feast with all the saints. In the liturgy of baptism we call upon Mary, John the Baptist, Ignatius, Francis and Dominic, Catherine and Teresa, indeed, all holy men and women, to pray for us. We need their intercession so that we too might get caught up into the glory of God revealed in the risen Lord. The communion of saints knew the source of amazement: the love of God. They desire that we too might ground our wonder and amazement in the light, love, and life of God's grace.

Meditation: What part of the Easter Vigil causes the greatest amazement for you? What role does the communion of saints play in your spiritual life?

Prayer: Risen and living Lord, we stand in awe before the mystery of your resurrection. Give us the gift of wonder and reverence as we contemplate your love for us. Help us to see your glory in the empty tomb.

April 8: Easter Sunday

Easter Poetry and Song

Readings: Acts 10:34a, 37-43; Col 3:1-4; John 20:1-9

Scripture:
On the first day of the week,
> Mary of Magdala came to the tomb early in the morning,
> while it was still dark,
> and saw the stone removed from the tomb. (John 20:1)

Reflection: Sin and death! When all is said and done, we stand powerless before these devastating realities. Sin ruptures relationships and leaves behind a wake of guilt, shame, and broken lives. Death, that ubiquitous reaper, boggles the mind and has the appearance of such finality as to make human existence itself absurd.

It was into this human condition that Jesus came in the mystery of the incarnation. It was into this human condition that Jesus mounted the cross to redeem us from sin and broke the bonds of death through the mystery of the resurrection. In claiming to be the Resurrection and the Life, Jesus has set us free and has called us into a whole new existence.

Mary of Magdala, like all of us, had to deal with personal sin and the fact of death. When she came that day to the tomb and found it empty, we can only imagine what went through her mind, what she experienced in the depth of her heart. She, like Simon Peter and John, would be tested in faith but not for long, for all three eventually came to understand that Jesus had been raised from the dead.

In the Easter sequence we pray: "Christ indeed from death is risen, our new life obtaining. / Have mercy, victor King, ever reigning! / Amen. Alleluia." In this song of thankful praise we claim Christ as our redeeming Lamb, as the Prince of Life having conquered sin, as our hope and victorious King. When the mind falters in its understanding, we turn to poetry and song to express our faith. Only later can theology catch up and help our understanding.

This same poetry and song is found in our Easter preface: "It is truly right and just, our duty and our salvation, at all times to acclaim you, O Lord, but (on this night / on this day / in this time) above all to laud you yet more gloriously, when Christ our Passover has been sacrificed. For he is the true Lamb who has taken away the sins of the world; by dying he has destroyed our death, and by rising, restored our life." This is our faith; this is the faith of the church.

Meditation: How does the Easter feast affect your daily life? In praying the sequence and the preface for Easter, what do you experience in your heart?

Prayer: Risen and loving Lord, deepen our faith in your presence among us today. May we understand more fully your presence among and within us. As we face our sin and the mystery of death, give us the gift of faith and hope.

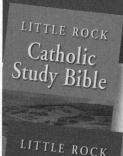